make me I'm yours...

sewing

compiled by Cheryl Brown

D&C
David and Charles
www.rucraft.co.uk

A DAVID & CHARLES BOOK

Copyright © David & Charles Limited 2010

David & Charles is an F+W Media
Inc. company

4700 East Galbraith Road, Cincinnati,
OH 45236

First published in the UK and US in 2010

Text, designs copyright © Alice Butcher
and Ginny Farquhar, Marion Elliot, Ellen
Kharade, Mandy Shaw, Sally Southern,
Dorothy Wood 2010

Layout and photography copyright
© David & Charles Limited 2010

Alice Butcher and Ginny Farquhar, Marion
Elliot, Ellen Kharade, Mandy Shaw, Sally
Southern, Dorothy Wood have asserted their
rights to be identified as authors of this work
in accordance with the Copyright, Designs
and Patents Act, 1988.

A catalogue record for this book is available
from the British Library.

ISBN-13: 978-0-7153-3772-1 hardback
ISBN-10: 0-7153-3772-6 hardback

Printed in China by Toppan Leefung Printing Ltd
for David & Charles
Brunel House, Newton Abbot, Devon

Project Editor Cheryl Brown

Designer Dawn Taylor

Photographers Kim Sayer, Karl Adamson,
Simon Whitmore and Stewart Grant

Production Controller Kelly Smith

Pre Press Stuart Batley

David & Charles publish high quality books
on a wide range of subjects. For more great
book ideas visit:
www.rucraft.co.uk

Contents

Introduction   4

Beautiful Bags   **7**
Pretty Oriental Purse   8
Oh So Versatile Handbag   14
My Best Jumper Bag   20
Girl About Town Carryall   30

Gorgeous Gifts   **37**
All Wrapped Up   38
Scent With Love   42
Music To Go   48
Fancy Stitching   52

Perfect Pillows   **63**
Quilt-Effect Cushion   64
Free As A Bird   70
Vibrant Cushions   76
Childhood Dreams   80

Techniques   89
Templates   110
Designer Credits   119
Other Books   120
Index   121

introduction

Are you one of the many thousands of women who have discovered that sewing can be a great outlet for your creativity? Do you want the opportunity to make chic and stylish projects unique to you? All you'll need is a little sewing savvy, some great fabrics and a few simple patterns to get you started.

Make Me I'm Yours... Sewing will take you from a needlecraft novice to an embellishment expert. There are twenty simple-to-sew projects to choose from, arranged into three irresistible sections. Beautiful Bags has fantastic designs for all your carrying needs, from pretty purses for party girls, to handy handbags for office angels. Once you start sewing, you won't want to keep your newly discovered talents to yourself. The present ideas featured in Gorgeous Gifts are designed for you to impress your loved ones, and include an elegant embroidered journal cover and a padded phone pouch for friends on the go. And finally, choose any one of the cushions with must-have stitch appeal included in Perfect Pillows to give your home that designer look.

The techniques section that begins on page 89 will guide you along the way. Look out for the techniques band feature at the beginning of each project – this lets you know the pages to turn to for the information you will need to make your chosen project. So what are you waiting for – choose a project and go fabric shopping today.

beautiful bags

pretty oriental purse

This simple-to-make little bag has more than enough room for your essentials — two side gussets mean that it is deceptively roomy despite its diminutive size. Finely woven cotton Japanese floral fabrics, used for the bag and its lining, perfectly complement the panel which adorns the bag front. For decorative detail, small buttons are sewn at the base of the handles.

A portrait of a geisha provides a wonderful focal point on the front of the bag. The geisha image is applied to a patch of plain green cotton fabric using transfer paste, and then edged with a ruffle-edged satin ribbon.

you will need ...

- 10 × 15cm (4 × 6in) plain cotton fabric
- image transfer paste
- paintbrush
- sponge
- 50cm (¾yd) patterned cotton fabric, 90cm (36in) wide, for bag
- 30cm (½yd) patterned cotton fabric, 90cm (36in) wide, for lining
- length of ruffled satin ribbon to fit around picture
- two buttons
- sewing threads to match fabrics

1 Photocopy the geisha portrait and cut it out. Following the manufacturer's instructions, paint transfer paste over the picture and press it face down onto the plain cotton fabric patch to transfer the image.

2 Dampen the back of the picture with a sponge and peel off the excess paper from the fabric. Leave to dry.

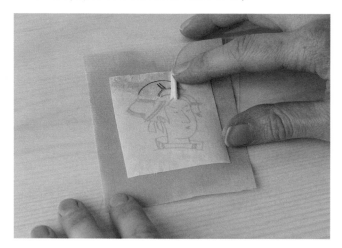

If you choose a reversible fabric for the bag as shown, the gussets, base and handles can contrast with the bag front and back.

3 Enlarge the bag body, base and gusset patterns from page 110. Cut out the pattern pieces: cut one front, one back, two gussets and one base from both the bag and the lining fabric. For the handles, cut two strips measuring 7 × 40cm (3 × 15¾in) from the bag fabric only.

4 Neatly trim the geisha picture and pin it to the centre of the bag front. Machine stitch the picture in place, using as narrow a seam allowance as possible.

5 With right sides together, pin the base to the bag front. Machine stitch using a 1.5cm (½in) seam allowance, to within 1.5cm (½in) of either end. With right sides facing, pin the gussets to the bag front. Machine stitch the gussets in place, to within 1.5cm (½in) of the bottom of the bag.

techniques basic sewing kit p. 90 ... using a sewing machine p. 95 ... slipstitch p. 101 ... sewing on buttons p. 109 ...
templates geisha portrait p. 111 ... bag body, base and gusset p. 110 ...

6 Pin the ends of the gussets to the sides of the bag base. Machine stitch in place to within 1.5cm (½in) of the end of the far side.

7 Machine stitch the ruffled ribbon around the geisha picture.

8 Pin the bag back to the gussets and base, and machine stitch in place.

9 Assemble the bag lining in the same way as the main bag.

10 Clip the corners of the bag and press open the seams. Turn through. Insert the lining, wrong side out, into the bag. Pin and tack (baste) the top edges of the lining and the bag together. Machine stitch. Turn over the top of the bag by 1.5cm (½in). Press under the raw edge and slipstitch the turning.

11 Press the handles in half, right sides together. Machine stitch along the side and one end, using a 1cm (⅜in) seam allowance. Clip the corners and trim the seams, then turn through the handles and press. Turn in the raw edges at the end of each handle and slipstitch the opening.

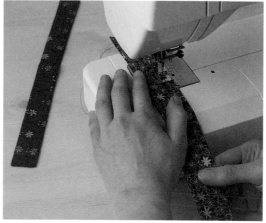

12 Pin the handles to the front and back of the bag, 2cm (¾in) in from the side seams. To secure the handles, machine stitch a square 1mm (¹⁄₂₀in) from the edge and finish with a line of stitching from corner to corner for extra strength.

13 Sew a button centrally at the base of each handle for decoration.

oh so versatile handbag

Fabric handbags are a wonderful way of accessorizing any outfit. Here a soft brown and green checked wool has been combined with real suede to create a smart everyday bag, but it is just as easy to make one suitable for a wedding or a special night out (see page 19). The bag is constructed in two pieces with a seam running across the bottom corners to give it more shape. If you prefer you can change the two shorter handles to a satchel-style strap.

For the bag shown here, the fabrics were sourced from charity or thrift store finds – a checked wool skirt with a silky lining and a suede jacket. The funky 3-D flower is finished with a vintage button.

you will need ...

- 30 × 80cm (12 × 31½in) checked wool remnant
- 30 × 80cm (12 × 31½in) lining fabric
- 30 × 80cm (12 × 31½in) canvas for interlining
- 15 × 16cm (6 × 6¼in) lining fabric for pocket
- suede jacket or skirt (not panelled) for handles and decoration
- scrap of plain wool
- double-sided fusible webbing (bondaweb)
- fabric spray adhesive
- one large button
- metallic magnetic clasp fastener
- sewing threads to match fabrics

1 Enlarge the bag body pattern from page 113 and cut out. Use the pattern to cut one front and one back from the wool fabric; two from the interlining; and two from the lining fabric. For the handles, cut two strips measuring 8 × 50cm (3⅛ × 20in) from the suede.

2 Using the templates on page 112, draw out the large and small flower motifs onto bondaweb. Fuse the larger one onto the suede and the smaller one onto the scrap of plain wool. Cut out, peel off the paper backing and fuse both flowers onto corresponding fabrics. Using machine zigzag stitch, sew round the edges of both flowers and put to one side.

3 Using the fabric spray adhesive, spray the canvas (interlining) and bond to the wrong side of the front and back pieces of the main body.

4 Place the small flower on top of the large flower and pin to the centre of the right side of the front bag. Starting at the middle point, using machine straight stitch, sew out approx 3cm (1¼in) into each petal to secure the flower.

Alternatively why not appliqué butterflies right across the front of the bag and along the straps too.

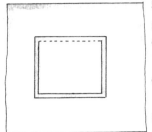

5 To prepare the inside pocket, turn over one of the longer edges by 1cm (⅜in), and press and turn over another 1cm (⅜in). Press and topstitch. Zigzag round the remaining three edges to neaten and then press under 1cm (⅜in). Pin into position (see body template) on the back piece of the bag lining, and sew a double row of topstitch around the three edges to secure.

6 To make up the bag and lining, pin right side front and back pieces together and sew the side seams and bottom seam of the bag using a 1cm (⅜in) seam allowance. Leave a 10cm (4in) gap in the bottom seam of the lining to turn the bag through. Press the seams flat.

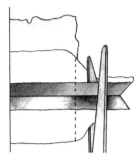

7 To create the base for the bag, and still working from the wrong side, fold the bottom bag corner open along the bottom seam, measure in 3cm (1¼in) and machine stitch a straight stitch at right angles across the width. Repeat on all corners of both the top fabric and the lining.

8 With right sides together, pin, tack (baste) and stitch the top edge of the bag to the top edge of the lining using a 1cm (⅜in) seam allowance.

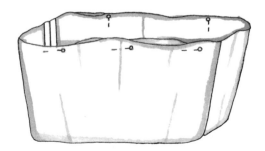

techniques basic sewing kit p. 90 ... using a sewing machine p. 95 ... using bondaweb p. 105 ... topstitching p. 97 ... understitching p.97 ... slipstitch p. 101 ... *templates* large and small flowers p. 112 ... bag body p. 113 ...

9 Turn through to the right side. Press the seams up towards the lining and understitch on the lining side (see illustration below).

10 Push the lining into the bottom corners and press with steam ensuring that you give the sides a crisp edge to create the side panels.

To prevent show-through on the bag front, insert a strip of canvas between the fabric and the clasp wings before pushing into place.

11 Take the handles and press the long edges under 1cm (⅜in). Pin and topstitch all the way around the edges. Press the short edges under 1cm (⅜in) and pin into position (see body template). Stitch a 2cm (¾in) square, 1mm (¹/₂₀in) from the edge, to secure each strap end and finish with a line of stitching from corner to corner for extra strength (see photograph above).

12 Insert the magnetic clasp following the manufacturer's instructions, before slipstitching the lining in place (see tip, left).

13 Finally sew the button onto the centre of the flower. Give the finished bag a final steam press.

beribboned evening bag

The handbag is so easy to make, you'll want to sew several to match your best outfits. This beautiful silk devoré evening bag is mounted onto pink linen and embellished with complementary beads. Rather than using a metallic clasp, a luxurious silk ribbon has been used to fasten the bag. Try creating a unique designer bag of your very own.

my best jumper bag

Nothing is worse than putting your best jumper into the washing machine only to take it out and find that it has shrunk to half its original size! This tendency for woollens to shrink in the wash is put to good use to make this stylish bag – rather than using your favourite jumper, buy one from a charity or thrift store. Look for knitwear with interesting patterns and features that you can include in the design.

This delightful corsage is the final finishing touch to the recycled jumper bag. It is so simple to make and the beads add a touch of luxury.

you will need ...

- old woollen cardigan or jumper
- stuffing
- two small felted balls (or button alternatives)
- patterned lining fabric (see step 10 for calculating size)
- set square
- two 25cm (10in) squares of synthetic felt in different colours
- fourteen small beads, 6mm (¼in) in diameter
- seed beads
- sewing threads to match fabrics

1 To felt the cardigan or jumper, place it in the washing machine with an old pair of jeans (the friction helps to speed up the felting process) and put on a 60°C (140°F) wash cycle with ordinary detergent.

2 Unpick the zip, if there is one, and discard. Carefully hand stitch the opening closed using neat little slipstitches. Cut off the arms at the seams and put them to one side.

3 Using dressmaking scissors, cut right across the cardigan or jumper, just below the armholes. Discard the top section.

This is the cardigan from which the bag was made. You can utilize any interesting features or patterns that your chosen garment has to offer – in this case, the front opening, pockets, contrasting ribbing and striped sleeves. The sides of the cardigan form the sides of the bag, so only the bottom edge needs to be stitched, and one of the sleeves is sewn to the top of the bag to create a decorative edging, while the other sleeve is cut in half to make the handles.

Make sure that your chosen garment is at least 80 per cent wool, as it may not felt sufficiently if there is too much synthetic fibre in the mix.

techniques basic sewing kit p. 90 ... slipstitch p. 101 ... using a sewing machine p. 95 ... sewing on beads p. 108
templates corsage p. 112

4 Turn the cardigan or jumper inside out and machine stitch along the bottom edge of the ribbing. The sides of the garment have now become the sides of the bag, so there is no need for any additional sewing.

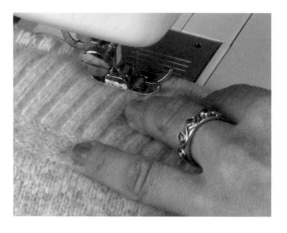

5 Cut one sleeve lengthways in half and trim one half until it is 4cm (1½in) wide and long enough to wrap around the bag plus a small seam allowance. Join the ends to make a ring. Discard the other sleeve half.

6 Pin the sleeve strip across the top of the inside of the bag and machine stitch in place. Turn the sleeve strip outwards over the top of the bag to create a collar. Curl the fabric under slightly, and sew in place along the outside of the bag using neat little slipstitches.

7 Cut the remaining sleeve lengthways in half and trim each piece to 9 × 44cm (3½ × 17¼in). Pin the long sides of one sleeve piece together and machine stitch to form a handle. Pinch off small wads of polyester filling and use a skewer to stuff the handle until it is nicely rounded. Machine stitch the ends of the handle to close. Repeat with the other sleeve piece.

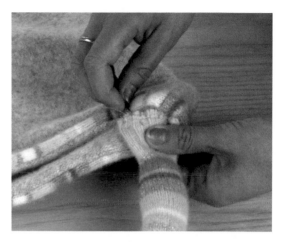

8 Measure 5cm (2in) from each side of the bag and 3cm (1¼in) from the top of the bag and pin each end of the two handles in place. Hand stitch each handle in position securely.

9 Trim an offcut of the cardigan to 2 × 12cm (¾ × 4¾in) and fold it over to create a loop. Secure the loop with a couple of stitches and then hand stitch it centrally onto the back top edge of the bag.

10 On the front of the bag, sew on a felted ball (or button alternative) in a corresponding position to create a fastener.

11 With right sides facing, fold the lining fabric in half. Measure the width and height of the bag. Using a set square, measure and draw out a rectangle the same size on the lining fabric, with the fold along the bottom edge. Cut out the rectangle, cutting through both layers of fabric.

12 Machine stitch the sides together, using a 6mm (¼in) seam allowance. Turn over and press down a 2cm (¾in) seam around the top edge. Push the lining into the bag and pin it to the inside of the bag just below the top edge. Slipstitch in place.

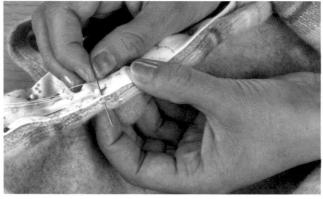

13 Using the corsage templates on page 112, make paper patterns for the flower centre and petal. Pin the flower centre pattern to one felt square and cut out. Using the petal pattern, cut out five petals from the other felt square.

14 Snip around the outer edge of the flower centre with embroidery scissors. Pinch each of the petals at the base to create a 3-D shape and secure with a few stitches. Assemble the corsage by sewing all the petals together at the base, then sewing the flower centre in position.

15 Sew the second felted ball (or button alternative) in the centre of the flower, then sew the small beads around the ball. Sew a cluster of seed beads to the top of the ball. Carefully stitch the corsage in place in the top right-hand corner of the bag.

fair isle bag

In this variation, the jumper was plain in style, so to add interest to the basic shape of the bag, the sleeves and neck were trimmed off, and the remaining fabric cut into two rectangles with inward-sloping sides for the bag front and back.

The Fair Isle pattern was striking and made it perfect for recycling into a bag.

A row of large coordinating buttons were stitched to the front of the bag for some contemporary-style detailing.

girl about town carryall

This simple bag is perfect for carrying your day-to-day needs to and from work. It's large sturdy shape is ideal for transporting your diary and stationery wallets, and a zip fastening keeps everything safe and secure. It is made out of tweed and wool fabrics in shades of heather purples and mossy greens. The mixture of different patterns and textures within the colour scheme adds interest.

Two roomy patch pockets are ideal for keeping pens and lipstick close to hand at all times.

you will need ...

- tweed-type fabrics in purple, brown and green tones
- double-sided fusible webbing (bondaweb)
- two large wooden buttons
- one medium wooden button
- purple zip, 36cm (14³/₁₆ in)
- sewing and embroidery threads to match fabrics

1 Cut two pieces of purple tweed fabric 28 × 38cm (11 × 15in). This will form the front and back of the bag. Cut another piece 10 × 90cm (4 × 36in) for the strap. Choose two brown fabrics and cut out of each a piece measuring 12 × 15.5cm (4¾ × 6⅛in) for the pockets. Put these pieces to one side.

2 Using the flower patch template on page 114, trace the outer flower, the inner flower and the flower centre onto bondaweb. Roughly cut out the shapes and iron onto the back of the fabrics you have chosen. Cut out.

3 Position the large flower at the bottom left-hand corner of one of the purple pieces of tweed. Peel off the backing and iron to fix in place. Fix the smaller flower onto the large flower in the same way using the photograph on page 31 as a guide to positioning. Finally, fix the circle in the centre of the smaller flower.

4 Use the green thread to sew around the edge of the large flower twice in running stitch; the purple thread to over-stitch around the edge of the smaller flower and to sew a running stitch border around it; and the brown thread to stitch the circle in place with catch stitch.

5 Sew small stitches along the centre of the small flower petals. In the middle of the circle sew a medium-sized wooden button.

6 Using the photograph on page 31 as a guide, make a pocket top pattern and draw onto bondaweb. Choose two fabrics and iron this shape onto the back, then cut out. Take the two pieces of brown fabric cut to be pockets and place the shapes you've just cut at the top. Peel off the paper backing and iron to fix in place.

techniques basic sewing kit p. 90 ... using bondaweb p. 105 ... running stitch p. 102 ... catch stitch p. 102 ... sewing on buttons p. 109 ... using a sewing machine p. 95 ... inserting a zip p. 99 ... *templates* flower patch p. 114

7 Sew around the bottom edge of the pocket tops in running stitch. Sew a large wooden button onto each pocket. Fold the edges of the pockets under by 1cm (⅜in) at the sides and bottom, and 2cm (¾in) at the top, then press with an iron. Hem the top edge with machine stitches.

8 Pin the pockets in position on the front panel of the bag and machine stitch around the three sides, leaving the top of the pockets open. Stitch along the sides and bottom of the pockets with green thread, and then along the top with purple thread.

9 Take the front panel of the bag, turn under the top edge by 1cm (⅜in) and press. Pin one side of the zip in position and sew in place. Repeat with the back panel.

10 Turn the fabric right sides together and pin around the remaining three sides of the bag. Machine stitch around the edges, leaving a 1cm (⅜in) hem. Turn the bag through to the right side and press.

11 Take the length of fabric cut for the strap and fold in half lengthways, right sides together. Pin the raw edges together along the length and then machine stitch. Turn the strap through to the right side, using a safety pin to pull it through. Press flat with the iron, then machine stitch down each side of the strap, 5mm (³⁄₁₆in) from the edge.

12 Fold under the raw ends of the strap and pin the strap onto the back of the bag, 4cm (1½in) from the top edge. Stitch the strap in place by sewing a square with a cross in the middle to make it more secure.

As an alternative to wooden buttons, use oversized shiny buttons in plastic or metal. They will catch the light and glint against the darker background.

gorgeous gifts

all wrapped up

What better to way to transform an everyday jotter into a desirable journal than with this simple-to-sew removable cover. All your girlfriends will want you to make them one. Choose a fabric that is resistant to fraying such as blanket fabric or heavyweight felt, and get ready to have a go at some easy stitchery for the simply stylish flowers.

Use a simple embroidery stitch such as stem stitch to work the stems and leaves, and then sew on a few wooden beads for the flower heads.

you will need ...

- notebook A6 size, 10.5 × 14.8cm (4¼ × 5¾in)
- A4 (US letter) sheet of paper
- 20 × 40cm (8 × 16in) wool blanket material
- black coton perlé No 5 and No 8
- twenty-one 4mm (³⁄₁₆in) black wooden beads

1 Make a paper template of the shape required by tucking the paper inside the notebook so the paper protrudes by 6mm (¼in) at the top and one side. Mark the other edges and then cut the paper 6mm (¼in) larger than the notebook all round.

2 Lay the blanket fabric on a cutting mat and use a rotary cutter (or sharp scissors) to cut a piece the exact size of the paper template. Cut two strips the same depth and 5.5cm (2¼in) wide for the flaps.

3 Lay one of the flaps at the end of the large panel. Thread a tapestry needle with No 8 coton perlé and inserting the needle from the flap side, work knotted blanket stitch around the edge of the flap. Tuck the book into the flap to check the cover is the correct length and trim slightly if necessary.

4 Stitch the flap on the other end in the same way. Continue to work knotted blanket stitch between the flaps on each side, and use a long enough length of thread so that you do not have to join the thread as there is nowhere to hide the ends on a single layer of fabric.

Work the knotted blanket stitch in a stabbing motion so the stitches are the same size on the front and back of the fabric.

5 Tuck the notebook inside the cover. Using the beaded flowers template on page 111, mark the design centrally on the front cover with a fade-away marker. Remove the notebook. Work stem stitch for the flower stalks and leaves along the marked lines using No 8 coton perlé.

6 Rethread the needle with the finer coton perlé (No 5) and sew a round wood bead just above each of the stitched lines, and then stitch a further six beads around each of the flower centres. Secure the thread ends on the inside of the cover to finish.

techniques basic sewing kit p. 90 ... using a rotary cutter p. 94 ... knotted blanket stitch p. 103 ... stem stitch p. 104 ... sewing on beads p108 ... *templates* beaded flowers p. 111 ...

scent with love

Scented decorations make the perfect gift – ideal for decorating the tree at Christmas, they can also be used to bring a pretty accent to a bedroom all year round. They are so easy to make from leftover fabric scraps. A selection of sumptuous silks, wools and velvets have been used here. Choose pretty cotton ginghams and checks for a rustic feel, or light floral prints for a feminine touch.

The project instructions show you how to make a bird-shaped decoration, but you could also try making other designs. Remember that the shape will need to work well when stuffed – strong, graphic shapes such as hearts and stars will work best.

you will need
for one bird
decoration ...

- two scraps of contrasting fabric for the bird and wing
- 24cm (9½in) 3ply jute gardening twine
- 45cm (17¾in) thin jute twine
- double-sided fusible webbing (bondaweb)
- sewing threads to match fabrics
- embroidery threads to contrast with fabrics
- stuffing
- dried lavender
- three glass beads with 2mm (1/10in) holes
- two 6mm (1/4in) buttons for eyes

1 Using the template on page 115, cut out two birds (one reversed) from the bird body fabric.

2 Using the template on page 115, cut two wings from the bondaweb. Fuse onto the wing fabric, cut out and press onto the centre of the bird body. Selecting a complementary embroidery thread, blanket stitch around each wing.

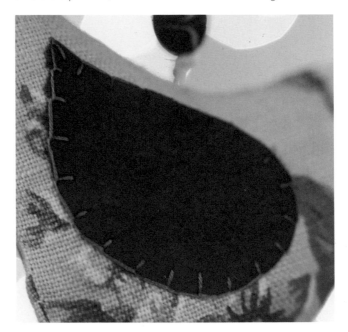

3 Take the 3ply gardening twine, fold it in half and make a knot. With right sides together, pin the bird inserting the twine at the leg position (see template). Using a 6mm (¼in) seam allowance, machine stitch all the way around, leaving an 8cm (3⅛in) opening. Take care not to sew over the long strands of twine tucked inside the bird.

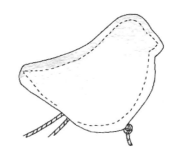

4 Clip the fabric at the beak and around the curves. Turn the bird through, paying special attention to the points at the tail and beak. Stuff the bird firmly, pushing the stuffing right into the points. Add a teaspoonful of dried lavender inside either side of the stuffing, pin and slipstitch the opening closed.

Use a knitting needle to push into the points. Don't be too vigorous, however, or you might make a hole or damage the seam.

5 Using a needle with a sharp point and a large eye, thread with the thin jute twine. Insert the needle at the bottom of the neck of the bird and pull through the twine so that you have a long length and a shorter length (about 8cm/3⅛in).

techniques basic sewing kit p. 90 ... using bondaweb p. 105 ... blanket stitch p. 103 ... using a sewing machine p. 95 ... slipstitch p. 101 ... *templates* bird p. 115 ...

6 Tie a double knot and cut off the excess twine on the shorter length. Thread the three glass beads onto the twine. Make a large loop (approx 12cm/4¾in long when doubled) and tie a double knot flush to the beads. Cut off the excess twine.

7 Finally, tie a knot in each of the twine legs (approx 3cm/ 1¼in from the body) and trim off the excess twine to approx 1cm (⅜in). Sew a small button to each side of the bird's face for its eyes.

Use the star template on page 116 to make luxury cinnamon-scented Christmas decorations as shown opposite. And for a wonderful Valentine's gift use the heart template to make a rose-scented heart, pictured right.

music to go

For anyone who has ever rummaged around in the bottom of a bag for their phone, sunglasses or mp3 player, they will be glad to receive this handy little gift to help them keep everything in its rightful place. Designed for an mp3 player, the finished size of this case is 13 x 6cm (5 x 2½in), and you may need to adapt the measurements to fit. Make a larger pouch for a snazzy sunglasses case.

Made from fleece fabric with a decorated fabric trim, this pouch will keep a mp3 player protected on the journey.

you will need ...

- fleece fabric
- plain furnishing fabric
- patterned furnishing fabric
- double-sided fusible webbing (bondaweb)
- large wooden bead
- ribbon, 3mm (⅛in) width
- sewing threads to match fabrics

1 Cut a piece of fleece 12 × 14cm (4¾ × 5½in), and a piece of plain fabric 8 × 14cm (3⅛ × 5½in). Pin the two fabrics together along the 14cm (5½in) edge and machine stitch.

2 Back the patterned fabric with bondaweb and cut out a decorative motif, in this case a flower. Peel off the backing paper and fuse in the centre of the fleece. Machine stitch to outline the decorative motif, starting with the centre flower.

3 Continue to outline the motif, stitching around each petal and finally around the edge.

4 Fold over the green fabric, leaving a 4cm (1½in) border above the cream fabric. Pin and sew 1cm (½in) above the join of the fleece and plain fabric.

5 Fold the panel of fabric in half, right sides to-gether, and pin along the edges, leaving the top open. Sew. Open the seam and press.

6 Turn through to the right side, and press flat. Cut a piece of ribbon 10cm (4in) long. Fold in half and sew the raw edges in the middle top on the back of the pouch so that you have a fastening loop. Sew the wooden bead onto the front to fasten.

techniques basic sewing kit p. 90 ... using a sewing machine p. 95 ... using bondaweb p. 105 ...

fancy stitching

This is the perfect gift for budding stitchers — a charming heart-shaped pincushion and an elegant sewing roll with lots of pockets and compartments for all those essential sewing accessories. The sewing roll features crazy patchwork created with an easy crazy stitch and flip technique, and the pincushion is really just two triangles sewn together.

Both the pincushion and the sewing roll are full of useful pockets to stash sewing tools. The same fabrics are used for both, and they are decorated with buttons, charms and oddments of ribbon trims and braid for a rustic look.

you will need for the sewing roll ...

- 50 × 25.5cm (20 ×10in) calico
- scraps of linen cloth
- ribbon trimmings
- 50 × 25.5cm (20 × 10in) thin cotton wadding (batting)
- 50 × 25.5cm (20 × 10in) check fabric for lining
- fat quarter of plain linen for pockets
- zip, 25.5cm (10in)
- 18 × 25.5cm (7 × 10in) polka dot fabric
- buttons and charms
- webbing tape, 5cm (2in) wide
- D-ring
- 4.5cm (1¾in) wide binding fabric, 152.5cm (60in) long
- popper fastener
- embroidery threads to match fabrics

1 To make the outer crazy patchwork panel, and using the calico as a foundation, crazy piece the scraps of linen (or linen-type) cloth using the stitch and flip technique. Decorate the crazy piece seams with braids, ribbons and lace.

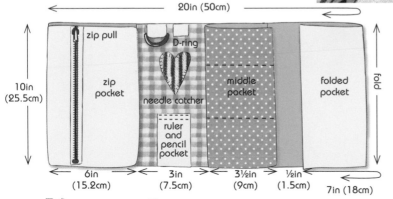

The interior anatomy of the sewing roll: refer to this diagram as you work your way through the steps to guide you when positioning the pockets and accessories.

2 Pin the wadding (batting) to the wrong side of the check lining fabric. Put to one side.

3 To make the zip pocket, cut two pieces of linen, one 10 × 25.5cm (4 × 10in) and the other 20 × 25.5cm (8 × 10in). Fold each in half wrong sides together, and on the folded edges, sew on a piece of plain tape or ribbon.

4 Take the smaller piece, put the zip under the folded edge and pin. Stitch close to the zip teeth. Sew another line 6mm (¼in) from the first.

5 Place the other folded piece on the right-hand side of the zip, making sure the folded pieces line up. Secure with a pin and sew close to the zip teeth. Sew another line 6mm (¼in) away from the first line.

Work with the zipper foot on your machine. You may have to undo the zip to allow the machine foot to pass the zip pull.

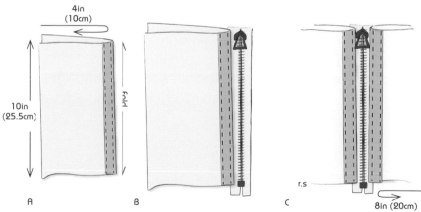

4in (10cm)

10in (25.5cm)

Fold

r.s

8in (20cm)

A

B

C

techniques basic sewing kit p. 90 ... using a sewing machine p. 95 ... crazy stitch and flip p. 107 ... inserting a zip p. 99 ...
sewing on buttons p. 109 ... ladder stitch p. 102 ... using bias binding p. 100 ... **templates** long heart p. 112 ...

6 Place the pocket on the left-hand side of the prepared lining, with the wrong side of the pocket to the right side of the lining. Make sure the zip pull is at the top and that the shorter side of the pocket is to the left. Pin in place. Attach the pocket to the lining by sewing a piece of tape or ribbon onto the right-hand side of the pocket.

7 To make the middle pocket, fold the polka dot fabric in half and decorate the folded end with ribbon or tape. Divide and mark the pocket into three sections measuring 8.25cm (3¼in), 9cm (3½in) and 8.25cm (3¼in). Measure a 7.5cm (3in) gap between the zip pocket and where the middle pocket will be and mark with a pin (see diagram, page 54). Place the folded end of the middle pocket on the mark. Pin in place. Sew the divisions through to the lining fabric. Sew on a ribbon or tape to cover the raw ends of the pocket and sewing-themed charms to decorate.

8 To make the ruler and pencil pocket, cut a strip of webbing tape 15cm (6in) long and decorate with ribbon and little heart buttons. Fold over the top twice and hem. Place the pocket onto the lining between the other two pockets and sew in place.

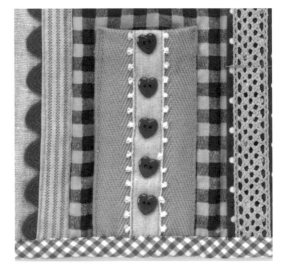

The linen-type cloth used for this sewing roll could include French tea towels, vintage fabrics, and even old embroidery.

9 To make the needle catcher, trace the heart (template, page 112) onto non-sew lightweight interfacing. Pin a piece of fabric slightly larger than the heart to the interfacing, wrong sides together. Sew on the marked line all the way around. Cut out close to the stitching line. Cut a slit in the interfacing, turn through and ladder stitch in place.

10 Cut a 10cm (4in) piece of ribbon or tape, fold in half and pin the raw ends to the top of the 7.5cm (3in) wide gap above the heart. This can be used to attach your keys to or for a cute bag charm. Make another with a D-ring attached for the same purpose.

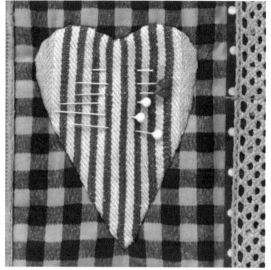

11 To assemble the roll, put the crazy patchwork panel on top of the lining, right sides together, and sew the right-hand seam. Open out and press the seam allowances to one side. Fold the crazy panel back and press. Ensure the crazy panel and the lining align trimming if necessary. Pin or tack (baste) the raw edges. From the lining side, fold over 9cm (3½in) on the right-hand side to make a final pocket (see diagram, page 54). Pin in place.

12 Bind the three raw edges of the sewing roll with 4.5cm (1¾in) wide single binding.

13 Cut a length of tape or ribbon 40.5cm (16in) long and attach it to the centre of the left-hand side edge of the crazy patchwork side and sew a large button on top. Fold over the other raw end and sew a smaller button on each side. This tape will wrap around the roll and fasten off around the button.

14 Decorate the finished sewing roll with simple embroidered motifs as well as the odd button and sewing theme charm. Sew a large popper on the right-hand side pocket to keep it closed.

Check out scrapbooking stores for great haberdashery, especially for collections of laces, braids, ric-rac and tapes.

15 To make a button pull for the zip, put some embroidery thread into the hole of the zip pull, thread on some small buttons or beads, and tie them off at the end.

16 To personalize the sewing roll, either appliqué fabric letter patches or embroider the recipient's initials on the outside or the inside of the finished project.

you will need for the pincushion ...

- 20cm (8in) square main fabric
- 10cm (4in) square pocket fabric
- five different braids, ribbons, ric-rac or lace, each approx 15cm (6in) long
- ric-rac or ready-made piping for outside edge, 50cm (20in) long (optional)
- stuffing
- ribbon or tape to decorate pocket, 25.5cm (10in)
- ribbon or tape for bow, 25.5cm (10in)

1 Cut the main fabric square in half diagonally. Fold the pocket fabric square in half diagonally and press.

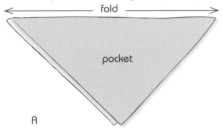

A

2 Decorate one of the larger main fabric triangles on the right side with ribbons, lace and braids; pin first to arrange nicely and then sew in place.

3 Decorate the top folded edge of the smaller pocket triangle with one of the 25.5cm (10in) lengths of ribbon or tape. Place onto the undecorated larger triangle and tack (baste) in place to make the pocket. You can decorate the outer edge with a length of ready-made piping or ric-rac if you wish.

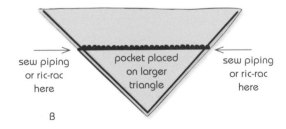

B

4 Place the main fabric triangles right sides together and sew around leaving a 7.5cm (3in) opening in the middle of the long edge.

leave
open

5 At each end of the longer side, squash the side seam onto the top seam (this is known as sugar bagging) and sew 2.5cm (1in) in from the point. Trim off the points.

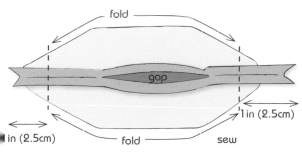

fold

gap

1in (2.5cm)

in (2.5cm)   fold   sew

6 Turn the right way out and stuff firmly, but do not stuff into the points. Close the opening using ladder stitch. Fold over both 'points' so they butt up to each other and ladder stitch together.

7 To finish, use the second 25.5cm (10in) length of ribbon or tape to tie a bow through the top of the heart to hide the stitching.

Stuff the pincushion with sawdust and put some lavender flowers or spices in too for a lovely fragrance every time you use it.

techniques basic sewing kit p. 90 … using a sewing machine p. 95 … ladder stitch p. 102 …

perfect pillows

quilt-effect cushion

This large cushion, designed to fit a 60cm (24in) cushion pad, is made by stitching together squares of fleece fabric to make a comfortable and cosy padded cover. The design is marked on the front of the fabric, then sewn using closely spaced lines of machine stitch to give a quilted effect. The final effect is a wonderfully inviting pillow for you to sink into at the end of a long day.

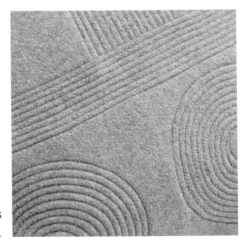

The simple, graphic design is made up of circles and lines.

you will need ...

- 70cm (28in) grey fleece fabric, 140cm (56in) wide
- compass
- 70cm (28in) pale blue fleece fabric, 90cm (36in) wide
- sewing thread to match fabrics
- 60cm (24in) square cushion pad

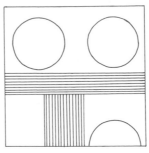

quilting diagram

1 For the cushion front, cut two 63cm (25in) squares of grey fleece fabric. Pin the squares together, one on top of the other, matching the edges and corners exactly.

2 Using a compass, draw a circle 20cm (8in) in diameter onto thin card and cut it out. Referring to the quilting diagram above, place the circle in the upper left-hand corner of the cushion front and draw around it with a fade-away marker. Repeat in the upper right-hand corner to make a second circle.

3 Machine stitch around the first circle using matching thread, following the pencil line. Use a long, straight stitch, otherwise the fabric will pucker. Complete the circle, place the machine foot against the stitching as a width gauge, and then continue sewing around to make a spiral pattern. Repeat for the second circle.

4 Mark nine equally spaced horizontal lines, starting 2cm (¾in) below the circles. Stitch along these to form a quilted band across the centre of the cushion.

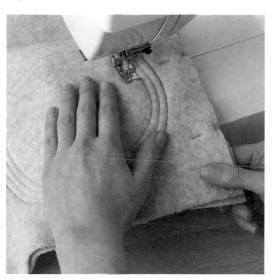

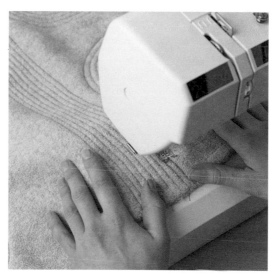

techniques basic sewing kit p. 90 ... using a sewing machine p. 95 ...

5 Starting 20cm (8in) in from the left-hand edge, mark and stitch fifteen equally spaced shorter lines at right angles to the quilted band.

6 Position the circle template in the bottom right-hand corner of the cushion, with the upper half overlapping the fabric. Draw around the template onto the fabric and stitch concentric lines as before.

7 To make the cushion back, cut two pieces of pale blue fleece fabric each measuring 63 x 40cm (25 x 16in). Turn under and pin a 1.5cm (½in) hem down one long edge of each piece of fleece and machine stitch using matching thread.

8 With right sides facing, pin one half of the cushion back to the cushion front. Pin the second half on top, overlapping at the centre to make a flap. Stitch the front to the back using a 1.5cm (½in) seam allowance.

9 Trim the cushion corners diagonally, just above the seam. Trim the seams (to avoid bulky edges) and turn the cover through. If necessary, use a safety pin to pull out the corners to sharp points. To finish, insert the cushion pad through the envelope opening.

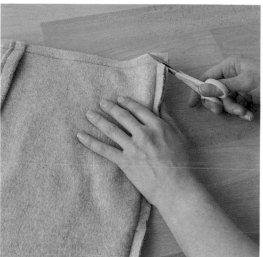

free as a bird

This comfortable yet stylish cushion features a bold appliquéd design worked in pretty floral prints on a richly coloured wool felt fabric. For ease and speed, bondaweb is used to attach the motifs to the cushion cover. Gold fringing, pearl beads and sequins have also been incorporated to add extra interest and sparkle.

This stylized dove motif is brought to life by cutting the body and wings from different patterned fabrics. The dove is set against a plain silk background for contrast and is decoratively framed with yet another toning printed fabric. Light-catching, jewel-like sequins and dainty seed pearls add an extra richness to the surface.

you will need ...

- 50cm (½yd) square wool felt fabric
- 50cm (½yd) square double-sided fusible webbing (bondaweb)
- compass
- 25cm (10in) square of four different patterned fabrics
- 25cm (10in) square silk fabric,
- fourteen sequins
- fourteen seed pearls
- 1.8m (2yd) of gold fringing
- sewing threads to match fabrics, sequins, seed pearls and fringing
- 40cm (16in) square cushion pad

1 Using a fade-away marker, draw a 40cm (16in) square onto the felt fabric for the cushion cover front. For the back sections, draw one rectangle 40 × 27cm (16 × 10½in) and another 40 × 32cm (16 × 12½in).

2 Using a hot iron, iron the bondaweb onto the back of each of the squares of patterned fabric and the silk fabric.

3 Using the templates on page 117, cut out a petal and a leaf from thin paper or tracing paper. Cut out the dove's body without the back and front wing. Cut out the back and front wing as two separate templates.

It is easy to dye old blankets to get the exact colour you may be looking for.

4 Pin the petal template to one of the patterned fabrics and carefully cut around it. Cut a total of fourteen petals. Cut fourteen leaves from a different patterned fabric.

5 Pin the dove's body template to another patterned fabric and carefully cut around the motif, keeping as close to the edge of the template as possible. Cut out the back and front wings from another patterned fabric. Fuse bondaweb onto the back of the silk fabric. Using a compass, draw a 18cm (7in) diameter circle onto the back of the silk and cut it out.

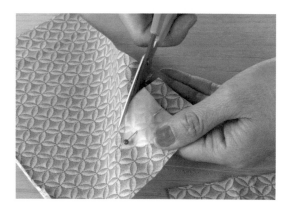

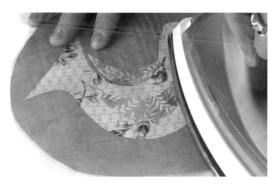

Choose printed fabrics in the same colour range to contrast with the felt, so the appliqué design shows up clearly against the background.

6 Peel off the backing paper from the bondaweb on the back of the dove and lay it on the silk circle, making sure that it is central. Use a hot iron to fix it in place. Attach the dove's wings in position in the same way.

techniques basic sewing kit p. 90 ... using bondaweb p. 105 ... sewing on sequins p. 109 ... sewing on beads p. 108 ... using a sewing machine p. 95 ... *templates* dove p. 117 ... petal p. 117 ... leaf p. 117 ...

7 Peel off the backing paper from the silk circle and lay it in the centre of the cushion cover front. Use the iron to fix it in place. Attach the petals in the same way, laying them slightly over the silk circle so that the corners of the petals touch one another. Lay the leaves in between the petals, fixing each one in place before moving on to the next.

8 Using a fade-away marker, randomly mark fourteen points over the silk background. Thread a needle with a length of thread to match and sew on a sequin at each point, knotting the thread securely.

9 Sew a seed pearl to the point of each petal, knotting the thread securely each time.

If a sequin has no hole in its centre, make one by placing a nail in the sequin's middle and gently tap it with a hammer.

10 With the front cover right side up, accurately pin the fringing around the inside edge of the fabric, with the fringing laying over the fabric. Carefully machine stitch in place, taking time to achieve a neat finish.

11 Fold over and pin down 2cm (¾in) along one long edge of each back cover piece and machine stitch in place.

12 With right sides facing, lay the slightly narrower back section over the front cover, then lay down the wider section next to it, overlapping by 15cm (6in) along the hemmed edges and aligning the sides. Pin the layers together, then machine stitch, taking a 6mm (¼in) seam allowance and making sure that the fringing is facing inwards so that the ends don't get caught in the seam.

13 Turn the cover right side out and insert the cushion pad through the envelope opening.

vibrant cushions

Arranged on the sofa, tucked in the corner of a favourite chair or strewn on a bed, cushions add a wonderful touch of colour, and no more so than these luxurious examples made from vibrant silk dupion. Longer and slimmer than standard cushions, they make the perfect support for your back or arms as you settle down to read your favourite book.

A gorgeous beaded panel decorates the front panel of this cushion, but you could just as easily use a wide woven metallic ribbon instead. Two alternative colourways are shown on page 79.

you will need for each cushion ...

- 28cm (11in) length of 4cm (1½in) wide linear ribbon

- fusible webbing (bondaweb)

- 50cm (½yd) silk dupion

- beaded panel, 7.5 x 25cm (3³⁄₁₆ x 10in) long (or ribbon alternative)

- sewing threads to match fabrics

- 30 x 45cm (12 x18in) cushion pad

If the silk is too lightweight to support the bead panel, back the fabric with a lightweight interfacing.

1 Cut the length of linear ribbon down the middle. Cut two strips of bondaweb and iron onto the back of the two ribbon strips.

2 Cut a 28 x 46cm (11 x 18in) piece of silk and fold in half across the width to mark the centre line. Pin the ribbon pieces either side of the folded line so there is a 4cm (1½in) gap between the decorative lines on the ribbon.

3 Pin the beaded panel across the silk so it is positioned centrally between the ribbon strips. Using matching sewing thread, hand stitch the panel onto the cushion cover top using small stitches every two or three beads.

4 For the cushion back, cut two silk pieces 25 × 28cm (10 × 11in). Turn over a 1.5cm (½in) double hem along the long edges; press and machine stitch. Lay the cushion top right side up. Pin the silk panels to either end with right sides together so that they overlap.

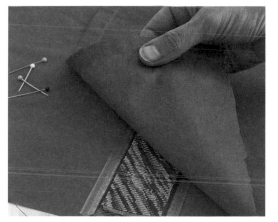

5 Using a zipper foot, sew around the edge of the cover and along the edge of the bead panel.

6 Trim the corners, turn through and press. Insert the cushion pad through the envelope opening.

Why not make a whole rainbow? Stunning pink and luscious lime versions are shown here.

techniques basic sewing kit p. 90 ... using bondaweb p. 105 ... using a sewing machine p. 95 ...

childhood dreams

This fairy cushion will delight girls of all ages, and, for the boys, there's a pirate alternative given on page 86. The simple patchwork border is the perfect opportunity to recycle fabrics, baby clothes and dresses that you can't bear to part with. Here a combination of pretty cotton floral fabrics were chosen, but the floral prints were kept small to avoid them overpowering the design.

The appliquéd fairy was created by using an embroidered blouse for her dress and gold lamé for her wings. These luxurious fabrics stand out beautifully on the simple plain linen background, and, for interest, the fairy is surrounded with simple hand-stitched stars.

you will need ...

- 17 × 17cm (6¾ × 6¾in) squares of twelve different floral fabrics
- 32 × 32cm (12½ × 12½in) natural-coloured plain linen for centre panel
- embroidered fabric for fairy's dress
- scrap of brown fabric for fairy's hair
- scraps of flesh-coloured fabric for fairy's face, feet and arms
- scraps of gold fabric for fairy's wings
- 62 × 62cm (24½ × 24½in) polyester wadding (batting)
- 1m (39¼in) of 140cm (55in) wide cotton calico lining or similar
- three 2.5cm (1in) cover buttons
- embroidered tablecloth or linen for backing fabric
- 60cm (24in) square cushion pad
- double-sided fusible webbing (bondaweb)
- fabric spray adhesive
- sewing and embroidery threads to match fabrics

1 Place the floral squares around the linen square. Starting with the top left square as number 1, work round clockwise and using tailor's chalk number all your squares from 1 to 12 on the reverse.

2 Using a 1cm (⅜in) seam allowance and right sides together, stitch square 2 to 3 and 9 to 8. Press seams open and, right sides together, place piece 2/3 at the top of the centre square and 9/8 at the bottom, and stitch. Press all seams.

3 Sew the side strips: 1, 12, 11, 10 and 4, 5, 6, 7. Press all seams and with right sides facing pin to the centre square, matching up the corners. Stitch in place, press and turn to the right side.

Re-arrange the squares until you are happy with the way they look.

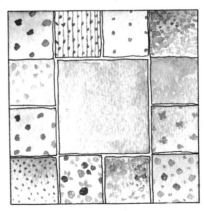

4 Draft up the fairy template on page 118 onto bondaweb. Fuse onto the wrong side of your fabrics and cut out. Peel off the backing paper and position onto the centre of the linen square.

If the fine machine appliqué seems a little daunting don't forget you can always hand stitch the fairy instead

5 Machine appliqué carefully around the edges with a matching sewing thread. Add the zigzag headdress, dress and wing details. Work French knots for the eyes and nose.

Fuse the complete fairy onto calico and cut out. Use this as a background shape to lay the smaller fabric appliqué pieces onto.

techniques basic sewing kit p. 90 ... using bondaweb p. 105 ... using a sewing machine p. 95 ... machine appliqué p.106 ... French knots p. 104 ... running stitch p. 102 ... star stitch p. 104 ... making buttonholes p. 109 ... sewing on buttons p. 109 ... *templates* fairy p. 118 ...

6 Cut a piece of wadding and a piece of calico lining to back the wadding, 62 × 62cm (24½ × 24½in). Using the fabric spray adhesive, spray the wadding and sandwich between the cushion front and the calico backing. Secure with a small running stitch around the outside edge just within the 1cm (⅜in) seam allowance.

7 With a contrasting embroidery thread, sew an even running stitch 2mm (⅒in) inside of the centre square. Embroider the star stitches in several different colours.

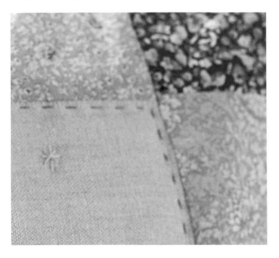

8 Now move on to make the cushion back. Cut an overflap and an underflap from the backing fabric, both measuring 62 × 42cm (24½ × 16½in). Cut facings from the calico lining, an overlap measuring 62 × 27cm (24½ × 10½in) and an underflap measuring 62 × 42cm (24½ × 16½in). With right sides together, and using a 1cm (⅜in) seam allowance, stitch the backing fabric underflap to the calico facing underflap along the long edge. Repeat with the overflap pieces. Press and turn with wrong sides together.

9 Mark three button positions on the overflap about 10cm (4in) from the bottom edge, with one in the centre and the other two approximately 16cm (6¼in) either side. Make the buttonholes.

10 To sew up the cushion, with the right side of the cushion front facing you (fairy right way up), place over the overflap (with buttonholes) and pin the raw edges to the top seam. Then lay over the underflap (without buttonholes) and pin the raw edges to the bottom seam. All right sides should be enclosed. Pin round all seams and stitch using a 1cm (⅜in) seam allowance.

11 Trim the corners, turn through the envelope opening and give a final press. Insert the cushion pad.

12 To make the cover buttons, cut three circles, 6cm (2⅜in) in diameter from the backing fabric. With the wrong side facing you, centre the metal cover button on top. Gently, with the point of some embroidery scissors, fold in the fabric securing into the teeth grips on the underside of the button. Snap on the cover button back.

It is a good idea to double back at the sides where the backing flaps meet to strengthen this potentially weak point.

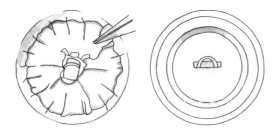

13 Attach the cover buttons to the underflap.

A beautiful linen tablecloth was used for the cushion back to complement the floral theme of the fairy cushion.

pirate pillow

Use the pirate template on page 118 to make this alternative for the boys in the family. It is based on a nautical theme, with a combination of reds, blues and greens taken from various checked and striped shirts. The backing is made from strips taken from salvaged jeans.

The pirate character really comes to life with a few carefully hand stitched details.

The nautical-style gold buttons embossed with an anchor make the perfect finishing touch.

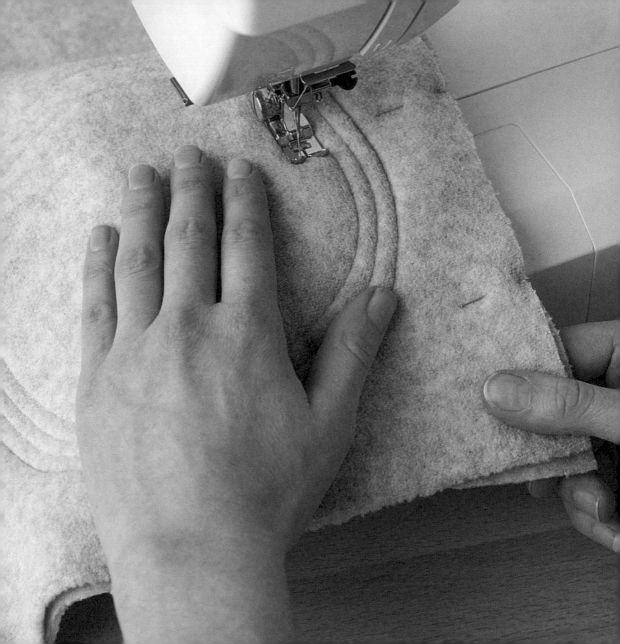

techniques

basic sewing kit

Each project in this book has its own You Will Need list, detailing the particular materials and equipment required to make it; however, the basic sewing kit details those additional items that you are most often likely to need as you work. Before you begin, do take the time to collect together the recommended items.

Measuring tools

• **Ruler (1)** for measuring or marking out and cutting against – ideally use a ruler with both metric and imperial conversions.

• **Tape measure (2)** Handy for measuring long lengths where a ruler is too short.

Adhesives

• **Fabric glue (3)** is quick and easy to use and is essential for attaching items that are too small or fiddly to stitch in place, or for sticking on ribbons and braids where you don't want to see stitching.

• **Fabric spray adhesive** is a useful product, as it temporarily places a fabric, thereby enabling you to move it around if necessary.

• **Double-sided tape (4)** will come in handy when you want to fix items temporarily.

• **Bondaweb**, a double-sided fusible webbing, comes in a roll or in pre-cut pieces. It looks like paper and is used to apply appliqué motifs and for joining pieces of fabric together permanently.

Scissors

• **Dressmaking shears (5)** for cutting out fabric.

• **Embroidery scissors (6)** have small sharp blades, ideal for fine work and intricate cutting.

• **General-purpose scissors** useful for cutting out patterns and general use.

• **Pinking shears** cut a zigzag edge that can be used to neaten seams or give a decorative edge.

Threads

A good quality thread is strong and elastic with a consistent thickness. Sewing threads fall into two main categories – practical sewing threads and decorative embroidery threads.

• **Sewing thread (7)** is used for sewing patchwork and for project assembly by machine or hand. These are easy to cut and sew and don't fray too readily. For best results, use a thread that matches the fibre content of the fabric you are working with and that is the same colour or slightly darker in shade. For tasks that require strong thread, you'll

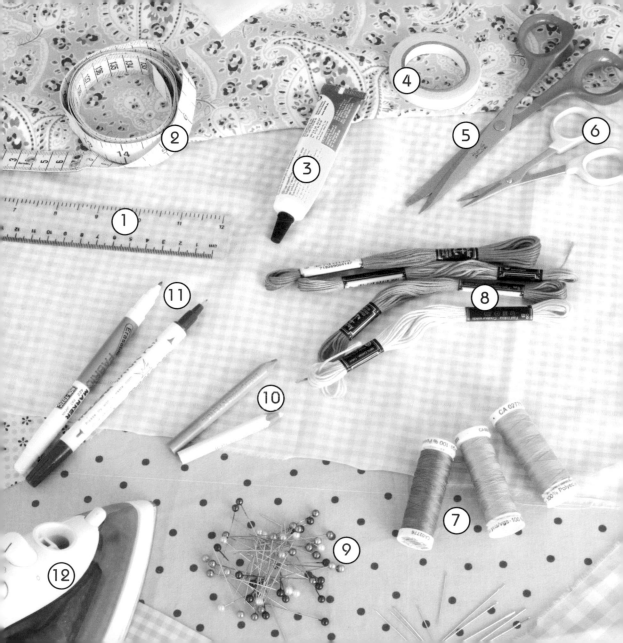

find buttonhole thread or topstitching thread useful. General-purpose polyester sewing thread is ideal for machine sewing and hand-sewing and comes in a kaleidoscope of colours.

• **Embroidery threads (8)** are infinite in their colour, variety and finish; they include stranded embroidery cotton (floss) as shown in the photograph on page 91, soft cotton, coton perlé, coton à broder and metallic threads for hand or machine stitching.

Pins

• **General dressmakers' pins (9)** keep fabric pieces in place before sewing. The colourful glass heads are easy to see against the fabric.
• **Extra-fine bridal and lace pins** are required for pinning delicate fabrics.
• **Safety pins** come in useful for turning through channels or pinning fabrics together.

Marking tools

• **Fabric pencils (10)** or tailors' chalk can be used to draw a line or pattern. The pencil marks rub off once the stitching is complete.

• **Fabric markers (11)** such as vanishing fadeaway markers are ideal, as they disappear after several hours on their own, or with a little water, so won't leave a mark once the sewing is completed.

Pressing tools

• **Iron and ironing board (12)** – see tip below.
• **Pressing cloth** this needn't be expensive – just a large square of muslin that will help protect your fabric and your iron.

Sewing machine

You will need a reliable lockstitch sewing machine that can sew straight and zigzag stitches. Utility stitches and a small range of embroidery stitches are also useful. A sewing machine will produce much stronger seams than hand sewing, and can be quicker and easier to use once you are familiar with it. See Using a Sewing Machine, page 95, for more information.

tip When pressing, the iron is pressed lightly onto the fabric, lifted and moved onto the next area. It should not be confused with ironing, which is when the iron glides over the fabric surface. Pins and tacking stitches should be removed before pressing and the heat settings adjusted on the iron according to the fabric type.

preparing for work

Before you start to work on your selected project, there are a few things you will need to prepare in advance. You will need to get together any templates listed for the project, make a pattern if necessary, prepare your fabrics for work, and mark, pin and cut out any fabric pieces. This section outlines a few essential 'getting ready' techniques.

Preparing patterns

Details of any templates required are given in the techniques bar at the beginning of a project. The templates are located on pages 110–118. Most are printed actual size, but a few need to be enlarged on a photocopier at the percentage given. If you need to make a paper template, you can pin it onto the fabric and then either cut it out around the template or use a fabric pen or pencil to draw around the template before cutting it out.

Pinning patterns

General dressmakers' pins are suitable for most fabrics, although silks and fine cotton should be pinned with bridal or lace pins. Pin the straight grain first, then pin around the pattern piece, diagonally at the corners and vertical to the pattern edge.

Marking fabrics

There are two ways to mark out designs onto your fabrics before stitching.

Using a fade-away pen

Any marks made with a fade-away pen will disappear on their own or with a little water. Use the pen to draw the line you want to follow with stitching. Once stitched, dab with a little water on your finger to remove any traces of the marks.

Using a fabric pencil or tailors' chalk

Any marks made with a fabric pencil or tailors' chalk will easily rub off once applied. Draw the line or pattern with the pencil and take care not to rub it out as you stitch. Once the stitching is complete, rub the pencil marks to remove.

Preparing the fabric

Prepare your fabrics by pre-washing them before use in mild detergent to check that the colours do not run and to allow for any shrinkage that might occur. If you are using a cotton lining or interfacing, you should pre-wash this as well. For delicate fabrics such as silk and wool that cannot be washed, you can gently tighten the fibres by hovering a steam iron 3–4cm (1¼–1¾in) above the cloth. Once you have completed this process the fibres shouldn't shrink any further. If the fabrics lack body after washing, iron while damp with a little spray starch, but be careful – too much starch leaves white marks on dark fabrics.

Cutting the fabric

It is always important when cutting out to have a clean, large flat surface to work on. Cut with the grain of the fabric, or if you are working with printed stripes and checks, cut with the pattern for best results. Always cut away from yourself.

Using scissors

Ensure that your dressmaking shears are sharp. To cut accurately, position your fabric to the left of the shears (or to the right if you are left-handed) and follow the edge of the pattern line, taking long strokes for straight edges and shorter strokes for curved areas.

Using a rotary cutter

The rotary cutter has a very sharp blade and is perfect for cutting out fabric into strips or squares, for patchwork for example.

1 Position a ruler firmly on top of your fabric and square off any uneven ends.

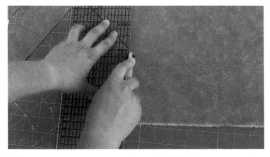

2 Turn your cutting mat through 180 degrees and line up the relevant mark on the ruler – e.g., 6.5cm (2½in) if 5cm (2in) is the finished size required (allowing for the seam allowance when sewing the fabric squares together). Line up your rotary cutter against the ruler's edge and cut.

using a sewing machine

Although it is possible to make most of the projects in this book by hand stitching, the sewing machine will produce a more consistent and stronger stitch, and you will be able to complete projects so much faster. It is well worth the investment if you intend doing a lot of sewing.

Getting started with the sewing machine

Take some time to read your sewing machine manual and become familiar with the different parts before you begin.

> **tip**
>
> It is always a good idea to test stitch on a scrap of your chosen fabric before beginning a project.

Presser feet

The presser foot holds the fabric firmly against the needle plate while the stitch is formed. It is important to use the correct presser foot for the stitch you are using and to test your tension on a scrap of fabric before you begin. Here are a few presser feet that you will find useful:

• **General-purpose foot (A)** for general sewing, utility and embroidery stitches on ordinary fabrics.

• **Zipper foot (B)** a narrower foot for sewing in zips and piping. The needle can be adjusted to sew on either side.

• **Clear view foot (C)** essential for accurate work as it allows you to see where you are stitching. It can be made from clear fabric or cut away. This is ideal for working on bulky fabrics and for machine appliqué.

Machine needles

Use an appropriate machine needle for your work and change it frequently – immediately if damaged or bent. Popular needle sizes are:

• **Size 70 (9)** for silks and fine cottons **(a)**.

• **Size 100 (16)** for leather **(b)**.

• **Size 90 (14)** for denims, canvas and heavyweight linens **(c)**.

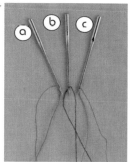

A   B   C

Preparing for machine sewing

Before you begin to stitch, it is worth taking the time to make sure your material is ready. Pinning and tacking (basting) are quick and useful ways of ensuring your fabric is lined up and stays in the correct place when machine sewing.

Tacking (basting)

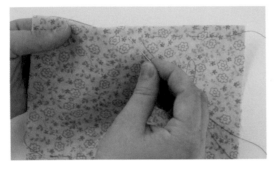

Tacking (basting) fabrics together will ensure that they stay in place as you sew them. You can remove the stitches afterwards. Using a thin thread, sew the fabrics together with large running stitches. When you reach the end of the fabric, do not secure the thread with a knot.

Once the fabrics have been sewn together, use an unpicker tool or a pin to pull out the tacking stitches.

Pinning

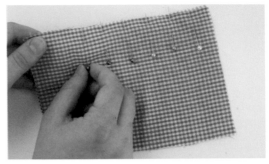

To sew two fabrics together by machine without tacking (basting), use this quick and easy technique. Place your fabrics together, edge to edge. Insert the pins at right angles to the edges of the fabrics, leaving a small even gap between the pins.

Stitch slowly over the pins – the needle will slip over each pin without bending them – and then remove the pins once the stitching is complete.

Machine stitches

The type of machine you have will determine the range of stitches available to you. Listed here are the main types of stitches that you will need to use on your sewing machine to complete the projects in this book.

Straight stitch (A)

All sewing machines will sew straight stitch and this is the type of stitch most widely used to join two pieces of fabric together. It can be used for sewing seams, topstitching and understitching. For ordinary fabric, set your stitch length to 3mm (⅛in) for tidy, even stitches. For fine fabrics use a shorter stitch length, and increase the stitch length for heavier fabrics.

tip If your stitches are different lengths, there may be a problem with your needle. Are you using the right needle for the fabric? Is the needle blunt and is it inserted properly?

Zigzag (B)

Zigzag is a versatile stitch, used to neaten seams and edges, as a decorative edge and to hold appliqué motifs in place. To neaten seams, it is best to set your zigzag stitch to 2mm (³⁄₃₂in) width and 2mm (³⁄₃₂in) length. When using for appliqué, set your zigzag to 2mm (³⁄₃₂in) and between 0.5 and 1mm (³⁄₃₂–¹⁄₁₆in) in length.

Understitching (C)

Understitching is used to keep facings and linings from rolling and becoming visible from the front. Trim back the seam allowances to 3mm (⅛in) and press to the side where the understitching is to be applied. Work a straight stitch from the right side and sew close to the pressed seam. The facing or lining can then be turned under and pressed and will lie flat.

Topstitching (D)

Topstitching is straight stitch set at about 3mm (⅛in) in length. It can be both decorative and functional, while holding the seam firmly in place. Place the presser foot onto the edge of the seam and use this as a guide to keep the stitching line straight.

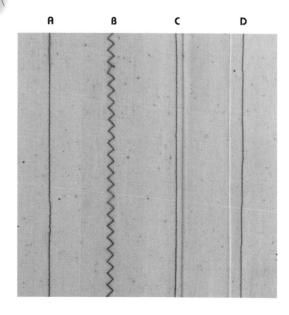

A   B   C   D

Satin stitch

Satin stitch is a zigzag stitch with the stitch length set at almost zero. It can be used to appliqué fabric patches, for buttonholes, and to provide a decorative effect. Check that the stitch width is right for the fabric before you start as satin stitch can sometimes make the fabric gather if the stitches are too wide. The faster you stitch, the more even your satin stitch will be.

Sewing by machine

The following basic techniques work to a 1.5cm (½in) seam allowance, which can be adjusted for each project as necessary.

Sewing a seam

One of the most basic tasks in any sewing project is sewing a seam.

1 Tack (baste) or pin the seam across the seam line, with the right sides of your fabric together.

2 Place your fabric under the presser foot so that the edge of the seam is next to the 1.5cm (½in) line on the needle plate and the fabric is 5mm (¼in) behind the needle. Use the hand wheel to take the needle down into the fabric, and then begin to sew.

3 Sew at a comfortable speed, guiding the fabric along the 1.5cm (½in) line on the needle plate.

Neatening seams

Finished seams can be neatened in a number of different ways to prevent them from fraying and becoming weakened – machine zigzagging the raw edges is one of the fastest. Try different lengths and widths of the stitch to find which best suits the fabric. Generally, the stitch should be as small and narrow as possible. Trim the seam to 6mm (¼in) and zigzag both edges together.

Turning corners

This is a basic skill that is essential when sewing more than one side of a project.

1 Stitch down the first length, leaving a 1.5cm (½in) seam allowance. Slow down as you approach the corner and use the hand wheel to complete the last few stitches.

2 Stop 1.5cm (½in) from the edge of the fabric, with the needle in the fabric. Lift the presser foot and turn the fabric around until the next seam is lined up with the guideline on the needle plate.

3 Lower the presser foot and continue to sew.

Sewing curves

A useful technique for stitching around curved corners or machine appliquéing shapes onto fabric.

- **For soft curves** Sew slowly, keeping the edge of the fabric opposite the presser foot on the guide-line of the needle plate.
- **For tighter curves** Stop and turn the fabric into the curve before beginning. Keep stopping every few stitches to adjust the line of the fabric until the curve is complete.

Inserting a zip

While it is possible to hand-stitch a zip, a machine-sewn zip will be so much more secure and will wear better. You will need to fit a zipper foot to the machine to enable you to sew as close to the zip teeth as possible, but you must be careful not to sew over the teeth, which can break the needle. Tack (baste) zips in place and allow 1.5cm (½in) seam allowances. Fold under the first piece of fabric by 1.5cm (½in) and pin it to the zip. The folded edge should be close to the teeth but allow the zip to be unfastened. Machine sew down the edge about 3mm (⅛in) from the fold. Sew the second piece of fabric to the zip the same way.

tip

Stop sewing at the zip pull with the needle down in the fabric, draw the pull past the part being sewn and continue stitching.

Using bias binding

Bias binding is used to enclose raw edges along seams on the wrong side of your fabric, particularly for quilts and bag linings. It consists of a strip of fabric cut across the diagonal to give the fabric stretch. You can purchase pre-fold bias binding in various widths, or make your own to match your fabrics following the steps below. Use a fabric that is of a similar or lighter weight than the fabric you are using for your project.

1 Cut 5cm (2in) wide fabric strips to the length required. Cut bias strips at 45 degrees (you can use the 45-degree angle on a quilter's ruler if you have one). Cross the two strips and mark a stitching line, then machine sew in position. Trim off the excess fabric and press the seam open.

2 Fold the binding almost in half lengthways and press the fold in place. Both raw edges of the binding should be visible as it is pinned and sewn in place, so any puckers in the fabric underneath can be eased out. Clip off the 'dog ears'.

3 Attach binding, pinning it to the edge of the project. Set the bias binding back from the edge. Machine sew the binding in place, leaving about 10cm (4in) of binding unsewn at start and finish. Open out the folded binding and join the ends with a 45-degree angle, as in step 1. Refold the binding and finish sewing it to the fabric.

4 Turn the binding to the back and stitch down using slipstitch. Take care not to twist the binding.

sewing by hand

The projects in this book use a variety of hand stitches for functional and decorative work, however they are all basic stitches that are easy to work simply by following the step-by-step photographs and diagrams given.

Hand-sewing needles

Choose a needle that matches the thickness of the thread you are using, so the thread passes easily through the fabric. You may need:

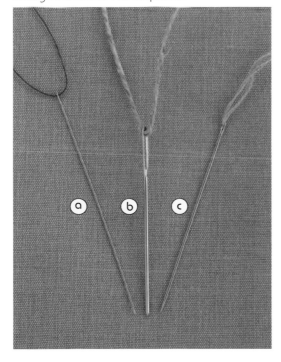

- **Beading needles** for beading **(a)**.
- **Large-eyed chenille needles** to thread twine for beaded decorations **(b)**.
- **Straw needles** – they are long and strong so will stitch through canvas or denim but are fine enough to bead and embroider with **(c)**.

Functional hand stitches

Take the time to get to grips with the two essential functional stitches – slipstitch and ladder stitch.

Slipstitch

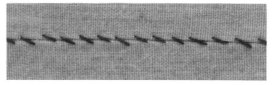

Slipstitch is used to hem, close gaps in seams, attach pockets and to insert linings. When worked neatly, it is an almost invisible stitch. Work from right to left, picking up a tiny piece of the fabric from one seam edge with the needle. Insert the needle into the other seam fold and move the needle along the fold 3mm (⅛in). Push the needle out into the seam edge and repeat.

Ladder stitch

The ladder stitch is a good way to close a seam on a stuffed item. It is so called because the stitches look like a ladder until you pull the stitches tight to close the seam. Knot the end of the thread and start from inside the opening so that the knot will be hidden. The stitch is generally worked between two folded edges. Take straight edges into the folded fabric, stitching into each edge in turn. After a few stitches pull the thread taut to draw up the stitches and close the gap.

Decorative hand stitches

Follow the simple diagrams and instructions that follow to master these decorative stitches.

Running stitch

This simplest of stitches, commonly used to attach two pieces of fabric together, can also be used decoratively, especially for outlining a motif, sewn in a contrasting thread colour. Working from right to left, simply pass the needle in and out of the fabric, making several stitches at a time and keeping the length even.

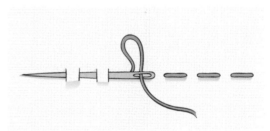

tip
For an even running stitch, make the stitches on the underside equal length, but half the size or less than the upper stitches.

Catch stitch

This simple stitch works effectively when sewing one piece of fabric to another, to appliqué for example. Tie a knot at the end of the thread and push up from the back of the fabric to the front, near the join of the two fabrics. Make a small stitch that overlaps the two fabrics in a straight line. Push the needle back through to the back of the fabric. Push the needle back to the front of the fabric a little way along from the first stitch and repeat.

Blanket stitch

Blanket stitch can be used to create a decorative edging and works best in a contrasting thread colour. Working from left to right, insert the needle into the fabric a little way in from the edge, the distance depending on the size of stitches you want, leaving the loose thread running down over the edge at right angles to it. Take the threaded end over the loose end and insert the needle a little way along the same distance from the edge as before; pass the needle through the loop of thread and gently pull up the thread. Pull the thread taut to form the stitch over the edge.

Knotted blanket stitch

This stitch is a more secure variation of blanket stitch where the thread is wound around the needle to form a knot at the fabric edge. Following the diagrams, bring the needle out of the fabric and make a 6mm (¼in) stitch through the fabric. Wrap the thread over and behind the point of the needle and pull the needle through to form a knot at the edge of the fabric. Make another stitch 6mm (¼in) further along and repeat the process.

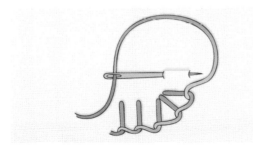

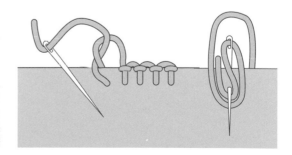

Star stitch

Push the needle up through the front of the fabric and down through it to create a stitch about 6mm (¼in) long, then bring the needle out to one side

to make a stitch over the first one, forming a cross. Continue to work the other diagonals in this way until you have a star with eight points.

Stem stitch

As its name implies, this simple stitch is often used in embroidery to create the stems of plants. Follow the diagram, first working a 6mm (¼in) straight stitch and then bringing the needle back out 3mm (⅛in) from where the thread emerges. Holding the thread loop to one side, pull the needle through.

Continue making 6mm (¼in) straight stitches, bringing the needle out on the same side of the fabric each time.

French knots

These are really useful for making small raised dots, for eyes for example. The weight of the thread will determine the size of the finished stitch. Bring the needle through to the front of the fabric. With the thread held taut, twist the needle twice around the thread. Pull the thread to tighten the twists a little, then, keeping the thread taut, insert the needle back into the fabric close to the exit point. Pull the needle through the twists to the back of the fabric.

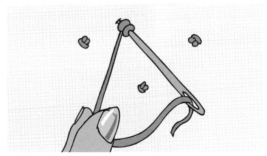

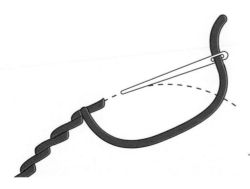

tip

Don't worry too much about your stitches all being exactly the same size or too neat as a slight unevenness can add to the quirky look!

appliqué

Applique takes its name from the French verb 'appliquer' meaning to apply. The technique involves cutting fabric to shape and applying it to a base or background fabric to create surface decoration, using either hand or machine stitching.

Using bondaweb

This double-sided fusible webbing is essential for applying appliqué motifs and joining pieces of fabric together permanently. It comes in a roll or in pre-cut pieces and looks like paper. One side can be drawn on and the other has a thin membrane of glue that melts when heated by an iron, so enabling you to attach one piece of fabric to another.

Applying bondaweb – method 1

1 Use a hot iron to press the bondaweb onto the

back of the fabric you wish to appliqué. Pin the template to the front of the backed fabric and cut out the outline carefully.

2 Carefully peel the backing paper away, position the motifs in place onto the base fabric and press with the hot iron to bond the motif in position.

Applying bondaweb – method 2

1 Trace the shape you want onto the paper side of the bondaweb. Cut out roughly, and iron it onto the back of the fabric you wish to appliqué.

2 Carefully cut out the shape and peel the backing paper away.

3 Place the shape onto the base fabric and iron to fix in position.

tip To avoid a sticky mess on your iron, be careful to iron only the paper side of the bondaweb.

Hand appliqué

For thin fabrics using bondaweb will be sufficient to hold the stitches in place. However, when using cotton fabrics for appliqué, extra stitching will be required in addition to the bondaweb. Decorative stitches such as running stitch, catch stitch and blanket stitch (see pages 102–103) are all perfect for the job.

Machine appliqué

Using a machine straight stitch or a close-set zigzag stitch or satin stitch to apply a fabric motif is an alternative to hand stitching. This will give a secure and durable finish that is ideal for items that will be washed frequently.

The heart appliqué is held in place with machine straight stitch. The less than perfect stitching adds to the charm.

Here the fabric motif is secured by carefully stitching around its outside edge with a machine zigzag stitch set at 2mm (³⁄₃₂in) width and 0.5mm–1mm (¹⁄₆₄–¹⁄₃₂in) length.

Stitching curves

When working on curved motifs, stop on the outside edge, needle down, foot up, and then turn the fabric. To ensure a neat result, it is better to stop and start several times than try to get around the corner in one attempt.

Crazy stitch and flip

This is an easy way to piece together patches for a crazy patchwork look and is used for the sewing roll on page 54. You will need a foundation fabric, such as calico, and assorted strips or pieces of fabric.

1 Starting with a fabric square, roughly cut off all the corners. Lay the fabric patch on the foundation fabric, then lay a strip of fabric along one

edge of it, right sides together, raw edges matching. Sew in place, trim off the extra length of the second fabric and flip it so that it is right side up, and press.

2 Now place a different strip or chunk on an adjacent edge of the multi-sided patch. Pin and sew in place as before. Trim the excess, flip the new fabric to the right side and press.

3 Continue to sew all the way around the multi-sided patch in the same way to cover the middle section of the calico. Vary the angles at which you sew the patches to achieve a non-uniform effect.

4 If there are any gaps that a strip won't cover, cut a square, turn under 6mm (¼in) on three sides (leaving the side hanging off the calico un-hemmed) and pin in place. Top sew in place.

5 Once you have covered all the calico, press and then trim the edges of the patchwork even with the calico.

embellishments

The addition of a button, bead or charm embellishment can provide the perfect finishing touch for your projects. Don't worry if you can't find exactly the same embellishments that have been used in this book – a personal touch will make your project truly unique.

Sewing on beads

Beads come in a vast range of colours, textures and materials, from delicate seed beads and pearls, to large hand-painted wooden beads.

Beading needles

These are longer and thinner than sewing needles with a flat eye to pass through the small holes in seed beads. Size 10 is a good standard size, but if passing the needle through a bead several times use the finer size 13. Beading needles bend or break easily so have a good supply.

Perfect beading

When sewing beads individually secure the thread carefully on the reverse when starting and finishing. Use a strong thread (quilting thread or a doubled sewing thread). Go through each bead twice to secure it. When stitching on larger beads, space the two threads out in the hole to hold the bead firmly in position. Take a tiny backstitch on the back before sewing on the next bead.

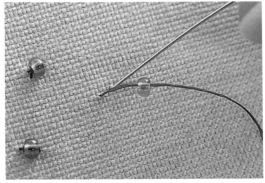

Sewing on seed beads.

Sewing on larger beads

Sewing on buttons

Buttons can be used as practical fastenings or as fun embellishments. Mix different types together and stitch on in different ways for a varied look.

Two- or four-hole sew-through buttons

 You can sew two- or four-holed buttons easily, either using two straight stitches or in a cross to apply the button to the fabric. Make a stitch where the button is to be positioned. Hold the button a little away from the fabric and sew through the holes into the fabric at least three times. Lift the button away from the fabric and wind the thread around the stitches. Finish off on the underside.

Shank buttons

Shank buttons stand slightly proud and are good for heavier-weight fabrics. To sew on a shank

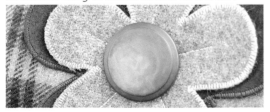

button first make a few stitches on the top side of the fabric. Hold the button slightly away from the fabric, and bring the thread through the hole in the shank and the fabric three times. On the last stitch, bring the thread up through the button and then wind around the stitches to form a shank. Finish on the underside.

Making buttonholes

Many modern sewing machines have a foot attachment that works out the size of the buttonholes for you and sews the buttonhole in one step. Older machines operate a four-step buttonhole. Check your sewing machine manual for instructions on how to create buttonholes on your machine. When you have completed your button-hole, take a sharp pair of embroidery scissors and cut down the centre line between the stitching, taking care not to snip through the stitches

Sewing on sequins

Sequins are so eye catching and can add a real touch of glamour to your design. To attach a sequin secure the thread with a knot. Bring the needle and thread up through your fabric and through the centre of the sequin, concave side up, to sew in place. Thread the needle back through the centre of the sequin again. Secure the thread once the sequin has been attached.

templates

All templates should be used actual size unless otherwise specified.

pretty oriental purse p8 enlarge by 220%

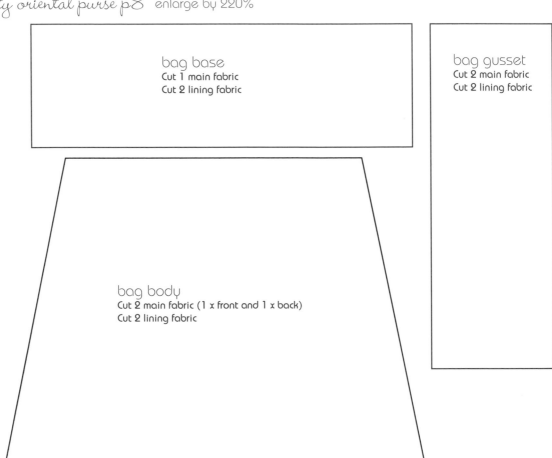

bag base
Cut 1 main fabric
Cut 2 lining fabric

bag gusset
Cut 2 main fabric
Cut 2 lining fabric

bag body
Cut 2 main fabric (1 x front and 1 x back)
Cut 2 lining fabric

pretty oriental purse p8
geisha portrait

all wrapped up p.38
beaded flowers

indicates position of beads

long heart

flower centre

petal

my best jumper bag p20
corsage

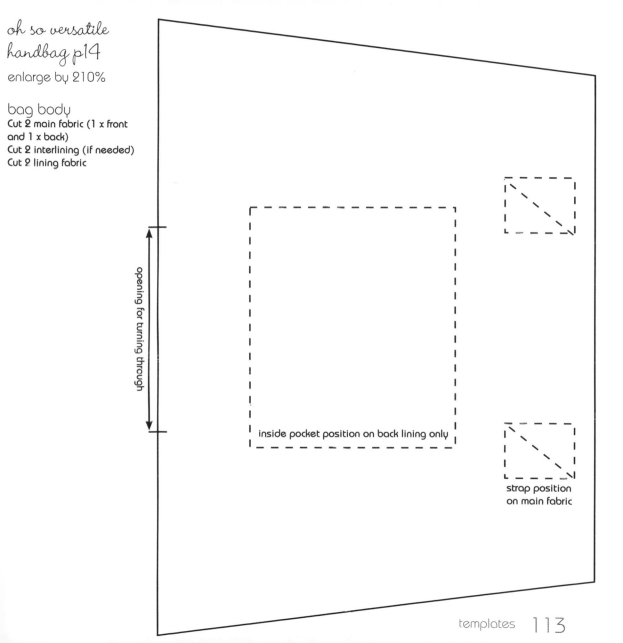

oh so versatile
handbag p14

enlarge by 210%

bag body
Cut 2 main fabric (1 x front
and 1 x back)
Cut 2 interlining (if needed)
Cut 2 lining fabric

opening for turning through

inside pocket position on back lining only

strap position
on main fabric

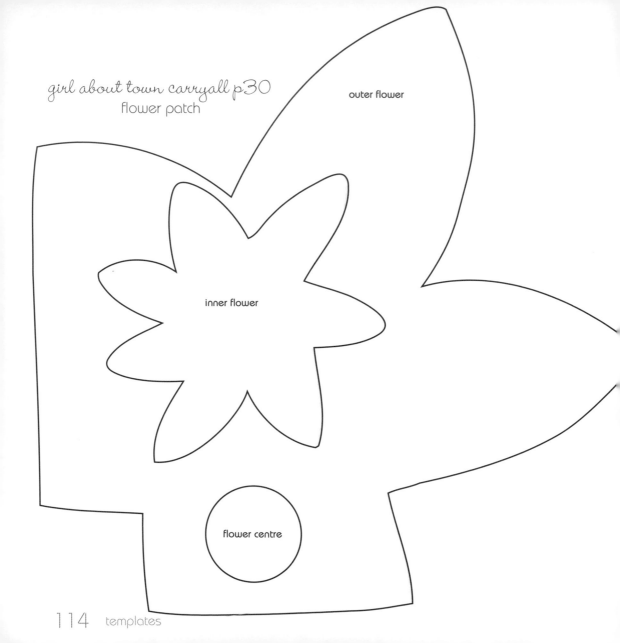

girl about town carryall p30
flower patch

outer flower

inner flower

flower centre

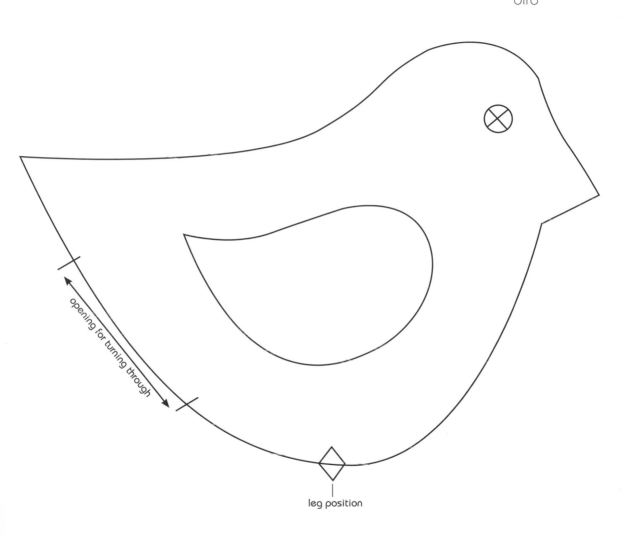

opening for turning through

leg position

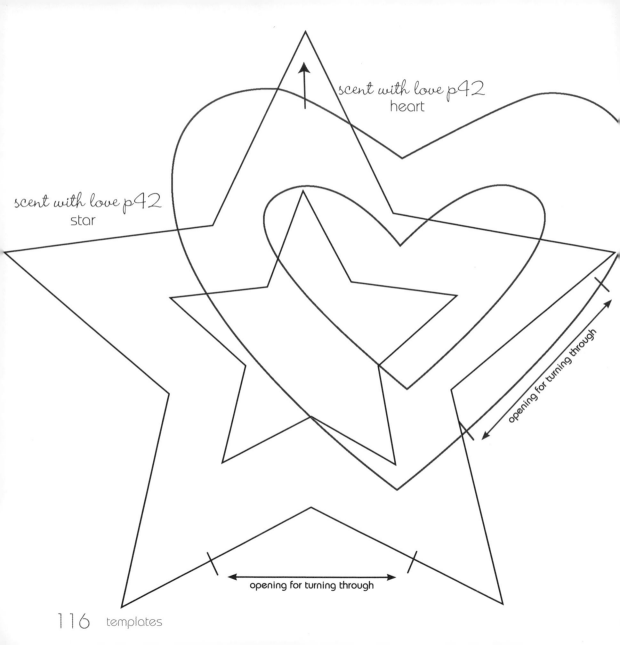

scent with love p42
heart

scent with love p42
star

opening for turning through

opening for turning through

free as a bird p70
dove

back wing

front wing

leaf

petal

pirate

fairy

designers credits

The publishers would like to thank the following designers who have allowed the reproduction of their designs in this book.

Alice Butcher and **Ginny Farquhar** for Oh So Versatile Handbag, Scent with Love, and Childhood Dreams.

Marion Elliot for Pretty Oriental Purse and Quilt-Effect Cushion.

Ellen Kharade for My Best Jumper Bag and Free as a Bird.

Mandy Shaw for Fancy Stitching.

Sally Southern for Girl About Town Carryall and Music to Go.

Dorothy Wood for All Wrapped Up and Vibrant Cushions.

index

A
appliqué 70, 80, 105–107
    hand 106
    machine 106

B
bags 7–35
    Beribboned Evening
        Bag 19
    Fair Isle Bag 28
    Girl About Town
        Carryall 30–35
    My Best Jumper Bag
        20–27
    Oh So Versatile
        Handbag 14–18
    Pretty Oriental Purse
        8–13
beads, sewing on 108
bias binding 100
bondaweb 90
    using 105
button pull 59
buttons
    cover 82, 85
    sewing on 109
    two- or four-hole 109

C
corsage 20
crazy stitch and flip 52, 54,
    57, 107
cushions, see pillows

D
D-ring 54, 57
decorations, scented 42–47

E
embellishments 108–109

F
flowers
    appliqué 50
    beaded 38, 41
    flower patch 33
    three-dimensional 14

G
gifts 36–61
    All Wrapped Up 38–41
    Fancy Stitching 52–61
    Music to Go 48–51
    Scent with Love 42–47

J
journal cover 38

M
mp3 player pouch 48–51

N
needle catcher 57
needles
    hand sewing 101
    machine 95

P
patchwork 80
pillows 63–87
    Childhood Dreams
        80–88
    Free as a Bird 70–75
    Quilt-Effect Cushion
        64–69
    Vibrant Cushions 76–79
pin cushion 52, 60–61
pins 92
presser feet 95

R
rotary cutter 94

S
scissors 90, 94
sequins 109
sewing kit, basic 90–91
sewing machine 92
    stitches 96–98
    using 95–100
sewing roll 52, 54–59
stitches 96–98, 101–104
    blanket 103
    catch 102
    French knots 83, 104
    knotted blanket 40,
        41, 103
    ladder 61, 102
    running 33, 34, 84,
        102

satin 98
slipstitch 101
star 84, 104
stem 38, 41, 104
straight 97
topstitching 97
understitching 97
zigzag 97
sunglasses case 48

T
techniques 89–101
    appliqué 105–107
    basic sewing kit 90–91
    embellishments
        108–109
    preparing for work
        93–94
    sewing by hand
        101–104
    using a sewing
        machine 95–100
templates 110–118
threads 90–91
    embroidery 91
    sewing 90

Z
zips 30, 54
    inserting 99